*"BUT IN THE END
YOU JUST HAVE
TO LET GO"*

OTHER BOOKS BY ROBERT M. DRAKE

Spaceship (2012)
The Great Artist (2012)
Science (2013)
Beautiful Chaos (2014)
Beautiful Chaos 2 (2014)
Black Butterfly (2015)
A Brilliant Madness (2015)
Beautiful and Damned (2016)
Broken Flowers (2016)
Gravity: A Novel (2017)
Star Theory (2017)
Chaos Theory (2017)
Light Theory (2017)
Moon Theory (2017)
Dead Pop Art (2017)
Chasing The Gloom: A Novel (2017)
Moon Matrix (2018)
Seeds of Wrath (2018)
Dawn of Mayhem (2018)
The King is Dead (2018)
What I Feel When I Don't Want To Feel (2019)
What I Say To Myself When I Need To Calm The Fuck Down (2019)
What I Say When I'm Not Saying A Damn Thing (2019)
What I Mean When I Say Miss You, Love You & Fuck You (2019)
*What I Say To Myself When I Need To Walk Away, Let Go And Fucking
Move On (2019)*
*What I Really Mean When I Say Good-bye, Don't Go And Leave Me The
Fuck Alone (2019)*
The Advice I Give Others But Fail To Practice My Damn Self (2019)
*The Things I Feel In My Fucking Soul And The Things That Took Years To
Understand (2019)*
Something Broken, Something Beautiful Vol 1(2020)
Something Broken, Something Beautiful Vol 2 (2020)
Something Broken, Something Beautiful Vol 3(2021)
Chasing Moons & Rainbows (2021)
*I WROTE THIS FOR YOU ME AND ANYONE TRYING TO FUCKING
MOVE ON (2021)*
BUT IN THE END YOU JUST HAVE TO LET GO (2022)
LOVE STORIES SUCK! (2022)

For Excerpts and Updates please follow:

Instagram.com/rmdrk
Facebook.com/rmdrk
Twitter.com/rmdrk

Book Cover: ROBERT M. DRAKE

For the broken For the beautiful
You know who you are

From the Author:

I know it has been some time. But I want all of you to know that since 2007 I have been writing every day for social media. Sometimes I feel like quitting. Sometimes I feel like I can no longer do this. It is hard on my mind. My soul and heart. I have been consumed by writing for a very long time. Sometimes I don't know where to begin. I don't know where to end. I don't know who I am anymore. I am trying to be better. I am trying to find a way out of my own darkness as many of you are. I feel alone most days. I feel a little dead inside, too. I don't know what it is that makes me feel this way. And I want to apologize for being so isolated with all of you who relate to my work so much. I am trying to be better but not just for all of you but for myself as well. Like I said, some days I don't know who I am anymore. I feel like a robot trapped in a vicious cycle. One with no end and I am not excited about anything lately. I feel troubled and very alone most days. But I am still here… trying to make the best of things.

I hope when you read this it really helps you. And I hope you feel better. I hope I feel better. Brighter days are coming. I know it.

*"BUT IN THE END
YOU JUST HAVE
TO LET GO"*

WHEN LOVE FINDS YOU AND STAYS WITH YOU FOREVER

You need love.

I don't care how hard
you want to be.

Or

how cold
you want to
portray yourself as.

You need it.

Everyone needs
someone to love.

Everyone needs
someone to be

vulnerable with.

To be real with—honest

you know?
So don't tell me
it's not for you.

As if
it has destroyed

your life.

Don't tell me
you don't need it

that you can live
without it.

That you've
"been there and done that."

You can't stay alone
forever.

Sooner or later
someone is

going to find you.

And they will
make you rethink
everything.

They will
convince you

to love again.

To want to take
that risk

again.

So don't
shut yourself out.

Don't say it'll never happen.

Because it will.
You'll see.

And it will be
unexpected.

As it always is.

And it will be
worth it.

You know it
and I…

know it too.

Please believe
in all the things

that are meant for you

even if
you cannot see them

right now.

WHEN YOUR MAGIC IS MORE THAN YOU THINK... IT BECOMES THE SUN

Who the hell
ever said

you were normal?

You have a million
different things

happening
inside of you.

A million
different feelings.

Colliding.
Fusing.

Bending.
Growing.

Shrinking.

My goodness
you are a gift.

A miracle.
A blessing within a blessing.

You're alive.
Right now.

In this very instant.

Making your mark
on a giant rock

floating through space
while rotating

a thousand miles
per hour.

And someone has the nerve
to call you

normal?

Shit

there is nothing
normal about you

or about that.

You are a gift.
You are

a marvelous blessing.

Take it all in.
Breathe it.
Feel it.

The magic you seek
is constantly

pouring out of you.

Let it flow
then come back

to it
in the morning.

And tell yourself

how rare
you truly are.

Because believing
in anything else

wouldn't make
much sense

at all.

WHEN YOUR BODY WELCOMES YOU... YOU ARE HOME AT LAST

You've been
at war with yourself

since the beginning.

It's time
to surrender.

Time to love yourself
for who you are.

And time
to believe

that although sometimes
things

do not go
your way

it is not
the end

but only
the beginning.

*Spend time
with this.*

*Spend your time revolving
around this.*

*Falling in love
with this.*

*This is your life.
And it is time
to welcome*

yourself home.

*You have been missed
for so long.*

WHEN TIME STOPS YOU WILL FIND THE LOVE OF YOUR LIFE AND THAT SAME LOVE WILL GIVE YOU LIFE

You know
relationships

are not easy.

They deserve time.
Effort.

And patience.

They deserve
mutual respect.

Mutual sacrifices
to make things work.

It's 50/50.

Give and take
and vice versa.

There should be balance.
Openness.
Understanding.

And did I mention
patience?

And more patience
and so on.

They're not meant
to be easy.

They're meant
to put us

on our toes.

Meant
to challenge us

in a positive
and respectful way.

In a way
we both can grow.

And learn
from each other.

We should be able
to trust each other

with our lives.

Be able
to rely on one another

when we feel down.
When we feel broken.

We deserve this…
this kind of love.

This kind
of connection.

But I know
it is not going to be easy.

I know
the journey

that's ahead of us
is an impossible one.

But we have to try.

Give it a chance
you know?

I mean
I can't see myself

doing anything else right now.

And I don't want to live
with regrets.

I don't want
to see myself

10 years down the road
wondering

about the possibility.

I want
to love you *now.*

And I want
to see where this goes.

Like I said
I know relationships

are not easy.

But I'm ready.

And I feel like I'm ready
to conquer the world.

I just want
to make it work

but I know
the road ahead

is a long one
and I can see

all the challenges
that lay ahead.

But I love you.

And that alone
is enough

to make a grown person
want to go through it all.

Alone or not.

I am willing
to make

things work.

WHEN YOU FIND WHAT YOU'VE BEEN LOOKING FOR IN A BOOK

No one can fix
what is unreachable

inside of you.

Only you
can do that.

Only you
can teach yourself

how to heal.

How to move on.
How to deal

with everything
you've been through.

*Only you
can save yourself.*

Only you
can find

what is meant for *you.*

Only you
can turn a bad situation

into a good one.

Into something
beautiful.

Only you
can give yourself

the clarity you need
to find the peace you need.

The people you need.
The love you need.
Only you.

You are your own salvation.
And no one can change that
but you.

SOMETIMES YOU WIN AND SOMETIMES YOU DO NOT WIN BUT IN THE END YOU STILL GROW

Sometimes
letting things go

is not the answer.

Sometimes
you have to face

what hurts.

Confront your fears.
Stand up to them.

Only then will you know
what you are capable of.

What you are made of.

Sometimes not running away
is the only way you
will grow.

WHEN YOU RECOGNIZE YOUR FLAWS AND WORK ON YOURSELF THE BEST WAY YOU KNOW HOW

Maybe
it's not them.

Maybe
it's you.

And maybe
it's time

for a change.

Don't be afraid
to blame yourself

sometimes.

Don't be afraid
to recognize

your flaws
and mistakes.

It is not
such a bad thing
to admit

when you were wrong.

It is not
such a bad thing

to want to learn
from your errors.

To want to improve
on such things

that need
improvement.

We all have them.

We all
experience this

 as we grow.

WHEN YOUR FRIEND LIVES IN YOUR BONES

Maybe what you need
is someone

to talk to.

Someone
who'll make you feel

understood
even if they really don't

understand you.

Someone
who's willing

to listen.

Who's willing
to just be there for you

even if

they have nothing
meaningful
to say.

Maybe
that's what you really need.

A friend.

Someone
who's not there

to fix you

but willing
to cheer you on

and support you

while you end up
fixing

yourself.

AMEN.

WHEN THE ANSWERS YOU SEEK FIND YOU, THEY STAY WITH YOU FOREVER

You don't
need them

to tell you
how they feel.

Their actions
will show you.

Their actions
will *always* let you know

how they really
feel about you.

Pay attention
to the details.

The answers you seek
will *always*

be found
in the details.

And they will
always define

where it is

their hearts
truly stand.

WHEN SOMEONE YOU LOVE LEAVES YOU BEHIND BUT THEY LEAVE A TRAIL OF FLOWERS TOO

Sometimes
you try everything

in your power
to make

the relationship work.

And sometimes
your best

isn't enough.

No matter what you do.
Some relationships

aren't meant to last.

Some relationships
are just meant

for you
to go through.
To experience love
and pain.

To learn
how to open yourself up

to someone
and soon enough,

learn
how to let
them go.

That's life.

Some relationships
are just

a chapter
in your story.

Nothing more.
Nothing less.

WHEN THE ROOTS OF YOUR SOUL PLANT THEMSELVES ON THE EARTH, LIKE THIS YOU GROW

Growth is admitting
when you were wrong.

Admitting
you have things

to work on.

Things you need
to learn

and things
you know

you wont understand
not until

you go through them
for yourself.

Growth is knowing

not everyone

will understand
your journey.

And knowing
that
too

is okay.

WHEN YOU SEEK HELP, SOMETHINGS JUST MAKE SENSE

Sometimes
the hardest realization

is

accepting the fact
that you don't

know everything.

That you still
have so much to learn.

And that
it is okay

to ask for help
when you need it

most.

WHEN THE TRUTH SURFACES AND YOU ACCEPT IT

The holy truth is

you will never
find peace

if you keep
running away...

if you keep
telling people

you are hard to love

and if you keep
telling people

you want to be alone.

Especially,

when all
you really want

is to be
loved.

Sometimes
the person you have

to let go of
is yourself.

Sometimes
you have to let go

of all that fear
you have within.

Let go of guard

and let
people love you.

Let people
give you

the love you
so dearly
deserve.

WHEN IT IS OVER BUT YOU STILL WANT THEM TO BE HAPPY... THAT IS WHERE YOUR LOVE WILL BE FOUND

Baby

if I never see you again

I want you
to be good to yourself.

I want you
to be good to people.

To love.
To laugh.

And try not to *overthink*
and analyze everything.

I want you
to follow your heart.

Even if it leads you

in the wrong direction

for a while.
I want you
to do

what makes *you* happy.

To live out your dreams.
To form new relationships.

To have as many friends
as you can.

I want you
to not lose hope.

To know
that tomorrow

is always brighter.

That tomorrow
is a new day

and that something better

is always within reach.

I also want you to know
that not everything
will be perfect.

Not everything
and everyone will be

as they seem.

But don't let that
discourage you

from finding
happiness.

Don't let that

discourage you
from wanting more.

From searching
for those perfect moments

that speak to us.

That make us
believe in magic.
In the goodness of things.

I want you
to keep going.

To keep digging.
To keep pushing yourself

towards greatness.

*Towards your own
kind of beautiful.*

I want you to smile.

To try not to let things
get to you.

To try not to let things
govern your heart

or get under your skin.

I want you to be free.

Like a wild bird
racing through the rain.

To be free
but *really free.*

To have full control
of your heart.

Mind.
Body.
And soul.

And to have them all
work together.

No matter how difficult
things get.

Sweet baby
I can write you

a longer list.

Because I just want you
to be proud of your life.

I want you
to find trust.

To find real connections.

To love deeply
and to have someone

give it back to you
in return.

I want you to live your life
without regret.

To live your life
without wishing

you can go back
and fix things.

I just want you
to live a life

you can be proud of.
One you can look back

and say you lived.
You laughed.

And above all,
you loved.

Freely.
Deeply.

And gently.

Stay beautiful
babe.

*I hope all
of your dreams*

come true.

WHEN YOUR DOUBTS TAKE OVER, YOUR MIND MAY BECOME A TERRIBLE PLACE

You are worth it.

And you do
have something

to offer.

Don't believe
in what fake

people tell you.

Don't believe
in what they make

you feel.

You are important.
You are beautiful.

WHEN TWO HEARTS MEET, THEY CONNECT IN THE MIDDLE OF THE SEA

I can tell
you're madly

in love with me.

And I hope
you realize

that I

am madly in love
with you
too.

WHEN IT IS REAL... IT WILL HURT AND THE PAIN WILL BE OUT OF THIS WORLD

You never
really know

how much you love someone
until

they're gone.

Until
they're completely unreachable.

The pain that brings
is like no other.

This is how you know
how much

you care.

HOW THE TRUTH SLOWLY BURNS AND HOW YOU WILL SLOWLY INHALE THE VAPORS

You love them
so much

that you are willing
to put up

with anything.

You're willing
to hurt yourself.

To put yourself
in the hardest

of situations *for them.*

And then
you wonder why

you feel
so alone sometimes.

Why you feel
so empty.

So confused.
So exhausted.
Of everything.

My sweet love
you have not learned.

The amount of time
and patience

you give them
should be what

you give
yourself.

You do not give
yourself the time

of day to grow.
You do not give

yourself the patience.
The dedication.

The love you need
and deserve.

Instead

you give it to the ones
who hurt you
the most.

To the ones
you want *to save.*

The ones you want
to heal.

My sweet love.

All of that energy given
should be given

to yourself.
And only to yourself.
AMEN!

WHEN YOUR SKIN BECOMES BULLETPROOF, NOTHING CAN HURT YOU ANYMORE

Mistakes happen.

Sometimes you do
something to the person

you're in love with

without thinking
about it.

You end up hurting them.
You end up making

things worse.

And you end up
retreating after.

But the beauty of being human is
that you can

realize
your mistakes.
You can
make things right.

You can
fix them.

Start over.
Heal.

You can acknowledge your mistakes.
Learn from them.

Grow from them.
And come back stronger.

Come back better.

That's what
coming out of the fire
is all about.

HOW YOUR HEART KEEPS YOU ALIVE

Just tell her
the truth.

Because nothing
is ever

really
permanent.

Nothing is promised.

All we have
is now.

And right now
you should tell her

how you feel.

And without thinking twice.

Always follow your heart

IT WAS ON MY MIND BUT I WAS TOO AFRAID TO SAY IT OUT LOUD

I just want you
to know

that I have never
felt more alive.

That I have never
felt anything more
beautiful

than all the times
I've spent with you.

You bring out the sun in me.
The moon in me.

And I have never
been closer
to myself.

And all because of you.
And only YOU!

SOMETIMES YOU HAVE TO START OVER WHILE YOU ARE STARTING OVER

Healing
is a strange process.

A delicate
little thing.

Like one day
you're completely okay

and then
the next day

any little thing
can take you back

to where you started.

Back to the beginning
of it all.

IT IS HARD TO FIND LOVE BUT WHEN YOU FIND IT HOLD ON TO IT FOR AS LONG AS YOU CAN

You are not
going to find

the "perfect"
person to love.

Not going to find
someone

with "all" the qualities
you've been looking for.

That's not
the way *it* works.

The trick is
find someone

who understands you.

Who's willing to learn

and adapt

to your flaws.

Someone who's willing
to accept your vices.

Who's willing
to look past

everything

and just love you
for who you are.

That's what
it's all about.

Finding someone
who's willing to accept you

no matter how fucked up
your past is.

Someone
who's willing

to be there for you.
Who's willing
to listen

and grow.

And vice versa.
That's what real relationships

are about.

About making it work.
About making it last.

And about
making sure

you both feel loved

appreciated

and understood.

It's as simple as that.

FLOWERS BLOOM THEN WILT
THEN BLOOM AGAIN

Just because
you're heartbroken

doesn't mean
you will

never love again.

You will.
You will learn

to love again.

And hopefully
this time

you take what you've learned
from your past.

And apply it.

So you don't let

the same mistakes
happen twice.

And you don't let
your heart

feel the same burn
again.

That's what
experience

and healing
is all about.

WHEN YOU FIND SOMEONE YOU LOVE THEY, TOO, BECOME TEACHERS

Maybe
it's not you.

Maybe
you have just

fallen in love
with the wrong

person.

Someone
who was never meant

for you.

Someone
who was just sent

to you
to teach you

something
you needed to learn.

Pay close attention.

Some ex's are teachers.
And they will teach you

some of the most
valuable lessons

you'll need to learn.

This is how
you'll grow.

WHEN YOU FIND SOMEONE YOU LOVE THEY, TOO, BECOME TEACHERS PT 2

Holding on to people
that are not meant

for you
will hinder your growth.

You must learn
to let them go.

You must learn
that although

they are a crucial part
of your journey

they are not
meant

to stay forever.

They're meant

to break you.

To heal you.

And to help you
make sense of it all.

I just hope
you're brave enough

to accept this truth.

To let go
when you must.

And to appreciate
people

for what they're meant
to teach you

and do.

WHEN YOU COME BACK TO THAT ONE PLACE YOU CAME FROM, EVERYTHING STILL FEELS THE SAME

I hope one day
we run into each other.

And I hope
we're old enough

to look back
and appreciate

what we had.

No matter how bad it ended.

I hope we're old enough
to understand

and admit
that we were *both* wrong.

That we were *both*

just two wild souls

looking for a chance
to love.

I hope we're old enough
to forgive each other

and I hope
we have a chance

to apologize
for all the pain

we might have caused.

SOMETIMES IT IS ONE SENTENCE THAT BREAKS YOUR HEART, SOMETIMES THAT IS ALL IT TAKES

And I felt you
deeply.

I felt you tenderly.

And that's why it hurt
that much.

BROKEN THINGS ARE SOMETIMES
A REFLECTION OF OURSELVES

The world is filled
with broken things.

Broken people.
Broken memories.

But it is in
our nature

to love them
as deeply

as possible.

THE BRILLIANT STARS WITHIN US

To help change
someone's life

is simple.

All you have to do
is care.

Love and be patient.

Sometimes
that's all it takes

to save
someone's life.

WHEN YOU ARE NOT SURE WHERE OR HOW TO BEGIN, REMEMBER... EVERYTHING HAS ITS PURPOSE... EVERYTHING WILL BE OKAY

It is okay
if you do not

have the words
right now

to express what you feel.

It is okay
if you don't

even know what it is
you are feeling.

It is okay
if you don't know

where to begin.

If you don't know

if a chapter in your life

has ended.
It is okay
if you are not sure

about your future.

Not sure
about your past.

About what you were thinking.

It is okay
if you suddenly fell out

of love with someone.

And especially
if you did not want that

to happen
but it did.

It is okay
if you don't know

how to apologize.

If you are not sure
if you even have to.

It is okay
if you wish

to move on.

Or even
if you wish

to stay where you are
a little longer

than expected.

It is okay to cry.
I mean to wake up

and *really* cry.
And or

to fall asleep crying.

It is okay
to wish you could
change things.

To wish you could
go back

and make all
the bad things right.

It is okay
if you are not happy

with who you are.

At least
not for the time being.

It is okay
to work on yourself.

To take as much
time

as you need

until you feel
comfortable in your skin.
It is okay
if you don't feel

the same.

Don't feel
the same

about certain things.

Like your career aspirations.
Certain people.

Certain places.

Certain things
 that used to speak to you.

It is okay
to move away.

To find new homes
within new people.

To find
what you love
in new places.

It is okay.

This is your life.
And only yours.

And life is too short
to worry about everything.

To *overthink*
about all the details.

Because it's okay.

And it's going to be
okay.

Just be yourself.
Just take your time.

Everything will be okay.

WHEN YOU MISS THE TRAIN AND HAVE TO WALK HOME

What else
can I say?

Sometimes life
is unfair.

You get
what you want

but not
what you need.

And sometimes
we learn this

the hard way.

Sometimes
we learn this

when it is
too late.

WHEN YOU FALL OFF A PLANE AND LEARN HOW TO FLY AT THE SAME TIME

I get it.

You want to please everyone.

You want to help
and save them.

But you can't
please everyone.

Sometimes
you just have to do things

for yourself.

Even if that means
complete isolation.

Complete solitude
and silence.

Sometimes

you have to take
a break from the world

and give yourself
the love you have.

Give yourself
what you deserve.

Even if there is no one there.

Find yourself.
Love yourself.

Notice yourself.

You cant save everyone
But you can

save yourself.

TWO TYPES OF PEOPLE, TWO TYPES OF LOVES AND THE BEAUTY OF IT ALL IS, YOU GET TO CHOOSE

You have something
they don't.

And that's why
they don't want

to accept you.

That's why
they try to put you down.

But you shouldn't
let them stop you.

You don't need
their validation.

You don't need
their hardness.

Their empty warmth.

Their hollow love.

The world is softer
because of you.

You make the people
who love you

believe in magic.

And that's
what should matter

the most.

Sometimes
you have to realize this.

How the people
who are still with you

are the only people
who matter.

The only people you
who deserve you.

The ones
who stay
and the ones

who will *never*
let you go.

WE CAN BOTH WATCH OUR FLOWERS GROW AND WE CAN BOTH MAKE SURE WE BECOME MORE THAN JUST WATER AND AIR

Maybe that's
what love is all about.

Finding someone
who will not only

water
the flowers in your soul

but also
teach you

how to water them
yourself.

Maybe that's what love is.

Two people
becoming air and water...
becoming more.

Becoming something
beautiful

for the whole world to see.

Let's makes a toast
and kiss the sky

in the name of that.

WHEN THE CARDS ARE LAID OUT RIGHT IN FRONT OF YOU, YOU MUST OPEN YOUR EYES AND TAKE THE TRUTH FOR WHAT IT IS

Sometimes
it is hard

to change yourself.

An impossible task
one

must sometimes try to do.

So imagine
how hard it will be

to change them.

Imagine
how hard it will be

to make them care.

To make them
treat you

the way you deserve.

Maybe it's time
to let go.

To stop
giving them more

of your time.

It's harsh to say.

But maybe they don't
deserve you.

You're too good for them.

It is you
who should focus

on yourself.

WHEN YOU CAN'T EXPLAIN IT BUT YOU FEEL IT, IT BECOMES A PART OF YOUR SOUL

Maybe that is why
we are drawn

to broken things.

Drawn
to fixing things.

Because the whole process
says more

about us
than we can ever say

about ourselves.

WHEN YOU LET SOME TIME PAST YOUR WOUNDS BEGIN TO HEAL AND THEY REMIND YOU OF WHY YOU SHOULD NOT GIVE UP

I hope you get over
your past.

I hope you move on.
I hope you heal.

I hope you find
the brighter days.

So when you meet
someone new.
Your past won't get in the way.

Your past won't influence
your actions and decisions.

And your past won't make you believe

that every new relationship will end the
same.

WHEN HE IS THE ONE, YOU WILL KNOW AND HE WILL KNOW AND ALL THE FRAGMENTS WILL MEND TOGETHER

Not all men
are cowards.

Not all men
are assholes.

Some are human.

And some can admit
when they're wrong.

Some can admit
when they know

they have issues
they need

to work on.

Some can be vulnerable.

Be real.

And be honest
with how they feel.

Not all men
are careless.

Not all men
are hard.

Some are soft.

Sensitive.
Gentle.
Kind.

But firm
when they must be.

Some actually want
to love.

And want
to spread love.

And that's it.

Some have been
through hell.

Been hurt.
Been dragged
on the floor.

Not all men
are the same,
love.

Some are different.

And maybe he does
love you.

So let him.

Maybe he does
want to show you

how much
he cares.

Let him love you
regardless

of your past.

I know
it is a risk
but it is a risk
worth taking.

Let him...

Let him show you
how not all men

are the same.

Let him be the one
who surfaces

and reminds you
of how

to breathe.

WHEN YOU SMILE BUT STILL FEEL EMPTY INSIDE AND WHEN THEY KNOW THEY DON'T BELONG AND STILL THEY CHOOSE TO STAY

Maybe if
you took the time
on her.

To listen to her.
To talk to her.

To let her express
how she really feels.

Then perhaps,
you'd understand.

ROBERT M. DRAKE

WHEN THE SUN INSIDE OF YOU SHINES SO BRIGHTLY, YOU CANNOT CONTROL WHAT YOU HOLD WITHIN

Perhaps

they will never
understand your value.

But that doesn't mean
you have to cut

yourself short.

Don't let them
make you feel small.

Never let the way
they treated you

make you feel
as if

you are worthless.

You are worth more
than you know.

More
than they
will ever know.

Stay strong.

Never let them
take

your shine away.

SPEAKING YOUR TRUTH IS AN ART, AND YOU MUST PRACTICE IT AS MUCH AS YOU CAN

If you don't
let them know

how you feel.

Then how will they know?

Never silence
your heart.

Especially
in the moments

when you feel
like

you have nothing left
to say.

BECAUSE THE WORLD IS FULL OF SADNESS BUT THAT DOESN'T STOP YOU FROM BEING YOU

You don't have
to be strong

for anyone.

You just have
to be happy

and comfortable
for yourself.

WHEN YOU FIND THE RIGHT ONE BUT YOU HAVE A LOT OF BROKENNESS WITHIN, YOU HAVE TO CHOOSE YOURSELF NO MATTER WHAT

Maybe it's me.

Maybe I'm
just afraid to love.

Afraid
to have someone

care for me.

Afraid
to get attached.

To always have to be there.

Maybe I'm just
not ready

to be loved—not ready

for a relationship.

Not ready
for someone
like you.

I'm sorry.

I have a lot of things
to work on.

I'm just not there yet.

I want to
but I know

I'm just not ready…
at least not now.

WHEN THE OCEAN SPLITS ITSELF IN HALF FOR YOU, YOU MUST MAKE IT THROUGH THE OTHER SIDE

*Don't worry about
what others think.*

*If it speaks to you
follow it.*

*And if it's meant to be
it'll find a way.*

IT IS BEAUTIFUL HOW THINGS HAPPEN: ONE DAY YOU WAKE UP AND EVERYTHING IS ALIGNED FOR YOU, EVERYTHING JUST MAKES SENSE

Love,
let them love you.

I know
you've been hurt.

And I know
you're afraid

to start over.

But you have to start
somewhere.

You have to take
the risk

all over again.

You cannot
live this way.

Cannot close yourself up.
Cannot believe
that everyone is out

to get you.

Love,
I know life is hard.

And I know people
are even harder.

But there's still
so much goodness out there.

So much love.

Believe me
when I say

your heart
will love again.

Your heart
will be mended.

Healed.
Forged.

Love,
good things are coming.

I can feel it.

Just make sure you're ready
for when it happens.

That's all.

SOMEONE ONCE TOLD ME THIS
WAS THE GREATEST SACRIFICE
PEOPLE MAKE IN ORDER TO LOVE

Some people
just aren't ready.

No matter how much
time passes.

They'll never understand
the type of sacrifices

you made for them.

They'll never understand
how long you waited

for them.

And they'll never.
Ever.

Understand
how badly you wanted

to make things work.

And how hard it was
for you

to let them go.

Some people just
don't know

how good they have it.
How good

others are to them
not until

several years later.

Not until
they are gone.

WHEN THE LOVE IS REAL IT WILL STAY WITH YOU AND IT WILL SHOW YOU HOW NOT ALL IS LOST

It doesn't matter
what stage

they are in their lives.

If they really
care for you.

If they really
want you in

their lives.

If they really meant
what they said.

Then they'll
make time for you.

They'll make you feel
appreciated.

And they'll make sure
you know
how they feel.

This is the great
balance of a relationship.

You give
and take
and vice versa.

You love
and show it

and in return
you receive

the same.

SOME MEN ARE STILL BOYS AND SOME BOYS WILL NEVER LEARN

*Don't inspire her
and don't open her heart.*

*Especially
if your intentions are
not to stay with her* ~

*If you intensions are
not to love her*

*and not
to grow with her.*

Leave her alone if that's not in your heart.

*Don't cage her.
And don't hold her back*

*from finding someone
who will make her feel*

like summer.

Who will make her feel
as if

someone
is always home.

WHEN YOU EXPECT TOO MUCH YOU FORGET WHAT YOU NEED, YOU FORGET WHAT MAKES YOU KEEP GOING

Sometimes
it is the expectation

that hurts us.

What we *want*
to happen.

How we dream it.
How we wish

for it
to unfold.

Or play out.

Sometimes
that's what hurts us

in the end.

It's not always people.

We expect too much
of them.

We anticipate too much.
And when things

don't go
the way we want.

We get hurt.

We break down.
We close up.

And we turn cold.

Expect less, my love
and let things be.

Expect nothing, my love
and let them be real.

Let people love you
the best way

they know how.

Let them light
a flame

in your heart
and let them remind you

out of all the things
you can possibly

love...

let the love
of another human be

the only thing
worth living for.

AMEN.

WHEN YOUR PAST HAUNTS YOU IT ONLY MEANS YOU CARE

It's true what they say.

You don't know
what you have

until it's gone.

Until you've had
so much time

to reflect
on what happened.

That you
yourself

wish
you could go back

and change things.

Go back

and do it all over
again.

But this time
pay more attention to her.

Give her more time.
More patience.

More kindness.

More soul.
More heart.

More understanding.
More love.

It's true what they say.

Sometimes
you just don't know.

Not until
it's gone.

Not until

you've realized
it's worth.

Until
you've realized

how much it really meant
to you.

That's life.

And sadly,
this is how we learn

to appreciate people.

By losing the ones
who meant the world to us.

The ones
we never thought

would be gone.

Lost
and out of our lives.

We regret
the mistakes we made

but we have learned
from those same

painful moments
to never to make

the same mistake twice.

So don't be
so hard on yourself.

These mistakes
must happen

in order for us to mature.

WHEN YOU SPLIT YOURSELF IN THE MIDDLE, YOU DISCOVER HOW BIG YOUR HEART AND SOUL REALLY ARE

I know you're trying
to save them.

But sometimes
the savior

needs saving, too.

Sometimes the healer
needs to be healed, too.

Take time for yourself, love.

I know you want
to help people.

And that's
a beautiful thing.

But you're neglecting

yourself

and your heart.
Save people.

But also
save yourself.

Love people.

But also
love yourself.

Find balance.

There is
no other way.

SOMETIMES THE EMPTINESS IS FILLED BY ANOTHER PERSON AND SOMETIMES THAT, TOO, IS OKAY

It's okay
to miss them.

Some people
know how to fill the void

inside of you.

They know
how to make you

feel good
about yourself.

Make you
feel at home

when all you feel
is lost.

Make you feel whole

when all you feel

is broken.

They're special.
They're rare.

They're hard to find.

They complete you.
And in ways

you can't explain.

In ways
no one can explain.

But
somehow

we all understand
the type of connection

they make us feel.

That type of love.

And that's why
you miss them

when they're not around.

That's why
nothing seems

to make sense
when they're gone.

They're just that different
from everyone

you know.

WHEN YOU HAVE NOTHING ELSE TO DO BUT LOOK FORWARD, YOU HAVE A LOT OF THINGS TO LOOK FORWARD TO

Sometimes
you just know

when it is over.

You just know
when you no longer have

anything left to give.

You just know
when you are ready.

To move on.
To start over.

To do everything
you must

for your own

well-being.

No matter how much time
you have spent together.
No matter how many memories
you have.

Sometimes
you just know.

And there is nothing
you can do about it.

When it is over, it is over.

And nothing can stop
the outcome.

Nothing
can make things go back
to the way they were.

All you can do
is accept this change.
Embrace it.

And know
there are still

some good times ahead.

Made in United States
North Haven, CT
22 June 2022

20533025R00070